All profits from this book wil
Anthony Nolan. Here's a little
work....

Anthony Nolan saves the lives of people with
blood cancer. The charity uses its register to
match potential stem cell donors to blood cancer
and blood disorder patients in need of stem cell
transplants. It also carries out pioneering
research to increase stem cell transplant success
and supports patients through their transplant
journeys. Everyday Anthony Nolan gives three
people a second chance at life.

Key facts

- About 2,400 people in the UK need a stem
cell transplant from a stranger every year
- 90% of donors donate through PBSC
(peripheral blood stem cell collection). This is a
simple, outpatient procedure similar to giving
blood
- Blood cancer is the fifth most common type
of cancer in the UK and the third biggest cancer
killer. It accounts for 9% of all new cases of
cancer diagnosed in the UK
- It costs £40 to add each new donor to the
register so Anthony Nolan always needs
financial support
- To join the Anthony Nolan register, you
must be 16-30 and healthy
- Anthony Nolan's world-leading Research
Institute has shown younger donors offer better
survival rates for patients

For more information, visit www.anthonynolan.org

In September 2021, my son-in-law was suddenly and unexpectedly diagnosed with Acute Lymphoblastic Leukaemia at the age of just 30.

He received – and continues to receive – epic levels of care from the team at Addenbrooke's Hospital in Cambridge. I wrote at the time that "like the ripples caused by a stone being thrown into a pond" the diagnosis turned their lives - and by association those of us closest to them - inside out and upside down.

In February 2022 Darren received a Stem Cell transplant, organised through Anthony Nolan and donated by an unknown 29-year-old man somewhere in the United States. There will never be enough ways to say thank you to him.

Treatment was brutal, recovery has been long and is ongoing. But we have Darren back. And now, *we* want to give back. We want to show how being on the donor register really does give people a second chance at life.

I hope that you find connection with some of the poems in this book. But, by buying it, you are enabling us to support Anthony Nolan in helping more people like Darren and give more families their loved ones back. And for that, I can't thank you enough.

Howard

The Hope We Cling To

How unpredictable life can be; how unforeseen.
Like a coin balanced atop a pin head
Ready to topple this way or that.
And yet how gritty and resilient too.
Courage will triumph over all our fears
Love from all quarters will provide the strength
to guide us through
As we walk together on this journey.
That's the hope we cling to.
You are the hope we cling to.

My Pledge

Don't love me out of duty
But because you want to.
Don't let my frustrations,
My many limitations
Restrict the lives you are able to live.
Some may tell you otherwise
But understand,
You owe me nothing.
There is no quid pro quo
Between past, present and future.
Honour what we may have had
By exploring, experiencing and living to the
fullest.
Then one day pay that forward.
I will never be a barrier to that.
That's my solemn pledge to you.

Heavy Is the Head That Wears the Frown

Another day
Another performance,
Treading water
Marking time.
Living, no
Just being.
Panic rises,
Chest tightens,
Breathing races,
Preparing to face
Each new day.
The looks,
The demands,
The threats
Of the everyday.
Aspire to solitude
Out of sight
Invisible
Untouchable
Unreachable.
It's not their fault
The ones I love.
They did nothing
To deserve this.
Watch over them
Keep them safe.
Heavy is the head
That wears the frown.

The Days of Our Lives

Think of the days when all you want to do is hide,
The days when every effort goes on feeling safe inside.
Think of the days when everything you see is coloured
black and white,
The days when the world seems to move around you, yet
nothing feels quite right.
Think of the days when you feel exhausted and every
sensation you have is numb,
The days when admitting you feel vulnerable makes you
think they'd think you dumb.
Now think of the days when once again you feel
refreshed,
The days when simple things like friends and family
remind you that you're blessed.
Think of the days when all you do is joke and share a
laugh
And look back on happy memories captured in a
photograph.
Think of the days when you can breathe in the air around
And nature's beauty, the birdsong and the solitude
abound.
Think finally of the days when you fail but still you strive
And recognise we all have good and bad days but it's still
a joy to be alive.

He Was All of Us

Some saw him as funny
Some, they thought him bright,
But no-one knew the real him
Alone in the dead of night.
No-one knew his hopes and fears
No-one felt his pain,
No-one saw as panic rose
And he wiped away the tears.
He hated the way it hurt him
And those who loved him most,
The ones who said they were there for him
Who said they'd miss him when he'd gone.
But who was he, this wretched soul,
This one with battles left unwon?
He was me; he was you; he was each of us.
He was someone's daughter, someone's son.

The Advice He Gave Me

The key to life is to nurture the soul
To feed it with love and keep it whole.
To cherish all who bring you calm
And banish those who would do you harm.
Remember, laughter always follows tears
And trust that hopes are stronger than fears.
Don't be afraid of the thrill of the ride
For every low there will be a high.
Be kind to yourself when you most need a friend
And know you'll be missed when it comes to an end.

Make A Wish

You can have one wish
The genie said,
So, make your choice with thought.
I mused on cars and holidays
And all else that could be bought.
I thought about a lottery win
And the fun that could be had
But the genie threw a sour glance
His patience wearing thin.
"It doesn't have to be for you,"
The genie said to me.
"You can make a wish for everyone
And who knows, it may come true."
When I told him what I wished for
I saw the smile across his face
"Make my wish come true, Genie
Make the world a kinder place."

Life In Colour

Help me understand the beauty,
Explain what I am missing.
Show me why you say it's precious
This thing that you call living.

Help me see the world in colour
And not just shades of grey.
Show me why you feel it's special
Before I fade away.

They say that each new day's a blessing
And still, I don't believe.
For me, the demons weigh me down
For what could have been, I grieve.

Reflections On a Manchester Night

They came to see their Songbird
To dance and jump and sing along.
To revel in the simple joy of being
Unknowing, as a cruel and twisted soul
Waits to silence the music
To shroud the lights in darkness and in blood.
And yet the night still turns to day
The world goes on again.
With pain in its heart and a tear on its cheek
Resolute, defiant, and with arms around itself.
So let the Songbird come and sing again
So, we can dance and jump for them.
So, we can shout 'We Choose Life'
And, for just a fleeting moment,
The innocents lost can sing and dance once more.

Once We Were in Love

When it's over and all that's left are the photos on your phone
Will you remember good times or just feel relieves to be alone

And when it's done and in the past and only memories remain
Do you think you'll hear my voice without it causing pain?

When the house is quiet by day and still of night
Will the hurt we caused each other make you feel contrite?

Will you let the hatred go and try to rise above
And let our children act as proof that once we were in love?

Peace of Mind

A cool breeze dances across the forehead
An unexpected gift in the early summer heat.
Awake yet still in the hush of dawn
Birdsong and traffic distantly embrace.
Secure in these protected surroundings
Alone with thoughts, once foolish dreams
Contentment teases with its temporary proximity.
Those most precious, safe, accounted for
And out of reach to those who are not,
Joyfully disconnected from the everyday
Yet, for just a heartbeat, fully alive in this world.

Love Letter to an Unknown Man

How can you love someone you've never even met?
Owe them more than they can ever understand?
What could possibly be expressed
To show him how much he means?
He probably thinks it was no big deal
But we know more than that.
How can you show enough gratitude
For giving back a husband, a son, a brother and a friend;
For giving back a life?

No Love

No love like the love in a child's eye.
Pure, and without condition.
In awe of those who gave them life
And first steps in a brave new world.
You are their hero.

No love like the love in a parent's eye.
Pride and passion entwined
In awe of the life created and unspoken possibilities.
Their hand clutches yours.
They are your world.

No disappointment like that in a child's eye.
Confronted by your imperfections.
Wide-eyed expectations narrowed by
Human limitation.
You, the hero, diminished.

No love deeper than a parent's loss.
When the nurtured need nurturing no more.
Inhabiting a world of their own
Adjacent; heroes now to others.
You, their bittersweet observer from afar.

No fear like the fear in a child's eyes.
Sobs unlocked from within the man.
The hardest thing to say is
Leave nothing left unsaid.
But how to let go, when
You, their anchor, works loose.

No tears like shared tears.
Memories recounted.
Raw and vulnerable moments in time.
And last steps taken together.
Your hand clutching theirs
Released, you leave their world.

Passing Through

Three in the waiting room
Together, yet alone.
A child paints rainbows on a blank canvas.
Curiosity incomplete.
A youth browses cars to remain forever undriven,
A lifestyle over before it's begun.
Not that he knows.
The older man is in the moment
He understands why they are there
And not among those left behind.
No time to say goodbye.
Together yet connected now.
Just like you and me,
Passing through.

When The Darkest Clouds Are Closing In

When the darkest clouds are closing in
It can be hard to catch a glimpse of the sun.
Your dreams can feel
Crushed like the leaves on the autumn pathway
Or lost in the density of the cold winter fog.
But cling on
For they will emerge again
Like the fresh shoots of the brand-new Spring.
The storm will have moved away,
Light and warmth to take its place
And we will love, laugh and smile again.

Choose Love

So much hate
That I just can't explain
Angry people with words
Designed to cause pain.
Religion, race, colour, sexuality
Thoughts laden with unbridled brutality.
How can you cling to such twisted views
Without seeing how they reflect on you?
What disturbs you so much
About the way others live?
What scares you so much
That such malice you give?
Stop for a moment, pause, rethink
It's never too late to step back from the brink.
Instead let no more hatred be hurled
Choose to leave a positive mark on the world

Dance To My Own Tune

To be left alone
To revel in the solitude and peace,
To breathe in deeply and feel anxiety decrease.
To disconnect from tumult and minimise the strife
To put an end to this restless, stress-filled life.
Just for once to not have to play the game
To live in peace and quiet, and be able to proclaim
That we shouldn't have to always do as everyone demands
But to dance to our own tune
Not to other people's commands.
To be left alone
To revel in the solitude and peace,
To breathe in deeply and feel anxiety decrease.

Come Together

These days it seems we drive our lives
Along different roads.
Though, who knows,
Perhaps one day
We'll part together once again.
And if and when those lives converge
You know our arms will still be open.
So, however you choose to get there
As long as we still have breath in our bodies
You'll find us waiting.

A Little More Time

All that we want is a little more time.
One more day to hold close to us
The ones who mean the most.
One more hour to say
All that we wish we had already said.
One more minute to feel the sun
On our faces and to breathe in the air.
And one more second
To blow a final kiss.
And yet all that we want
Is what we know we cannot have.

Move On

When you held my hand that one last time
And wouldn't release your grip,
I heard you whisper in my ear
And smooth your palm across my hair.
I felt your tears fall on my cheek
When you told me that you loved me.
I wanted to say I loved you too
But had no strength to speak.
I knew then it was time to leave
For me to pass, so you could grieve.
But promise me it's not for long
Only one life has run its course.
Move on, my love, embrace the world
It deserves you.

Life Is A Contradiction

How would it be to just slip away
To turn everything off and just leave one day.
Would your problems follow you
Or would you start to feel free
Before a sense of shame bore down
Overwhelmingly.

How might it be to for once feel alive
To wake in the morning
And believe you could thrive
Is that even possible
Or maybe it's fiction
Can life really be beautiful
Or is it just a contradiction?

Go Again

I hit a brick wall today
Not literally, of course.
But I felt bruised and battered
My confidence shattered
Burned out to the point
Where only ashes remained.
I sat on a bench
Blanked out all the voices.
Closed my eyes
And opened my mind
I relaxed my shoulders
And listened to sounds.
Treated myself to a latte
To warm up my hearty
And resolved to go again

Keep Smiling !

The pain, it ebbs and it flows
But never can you truly say
That it ever really goes.
Instead, it slips back
Into the recesses of your mind
Hiding in plain sight
Ready to revisit you one night.
Just as things feel calmer
And you think it's all behind you
It taps you on the shoulder
To remind you it's still there.
The fear, it also comes again
You never fully shake it off.
But nobody needs to know
If you keep that smile on your face.

The World Outside

Pull the curtains,
Shut the world outside,
Hide beneath the duvet,
So no-one hears your cries.
You can't conceal it any longer,
Think how you'll break the news,
Will it come as a shock to them
Or will they have seen the clues?
You think you'll go on forever,
But deep down you know that's not true.
Search and find some inner strength
For the moment truth confronts you.
All those times you stressed and stressed
Put work above all else
Now you can see what a waste that was
How it made you cheat yourself.
It's too late to change that now
Your life has run its course
But leave it just the best you can
And for love, remain the source.

My Safe Space

My bed is my safe space
My "they can't get me here place".
The bolt hole I revert to
When I need to disappear.

When I'm looking for sanctuary
For safety and security
I can pull the duvet overhead
And block the world outside.

But now I'm getting older
Crankier and bolder
Please can I ignore all others
And spend my days beneath the covers.

Proud

You make my heart burst with pride
Bring love to the surface I just can't hide.
You give me the reason to go again
Instead of laying down and giving in.
You're the ones who put a smile on my face
You're the ones who root me in this place
All I want is to see you soar
I honestly couldn't love you more.

Keep On Keeping On

From the highs to the lows
Through the ebbs and the flows
Just keep on keeping on.

To the child who screams
And the young man with dreams
Be sure to keep believing.

To the couple weighed down
By stress-laden frowns
Who stay focused on what's really important

It's those who are closest
Who matter the mostest
And will being you the joy that you need

So, channel your energy
To overcome lethargy
And refuse to be held back by others

You don't have much time
To make your life here sublime
So, live it the way that you want to.

Tiredness, take me

Have you reached the age
When your body just won't do
What your mind wants it to?
When your back has you walking
Like you're already in the care home
To the amusement of those around you.
When your idea of a great night
Is crawling under the duvet
With a book before ten.
Have you reached that age when
Turning over in the night
Creates noises loud and strange enough
To be your latest concept album?
When a special day out
Means Waitrose not Tesco
For a coffee in the cafe,
Decaffeinated, of course.
Have you reached the age
When you'd give anything
To climb off of the hamster's wheel
And press pause for a month or three?
Or when even surrounded by people
You can sometimes feel like
The loneliest person in the world,
Tempted to power off rather than power down.
You haven't?
You will.
It comes to us all.

It Is What It Is

Awake again
Marking time.
The fear of one
Resolute against the hope of others.
How it is
Is not how it is supposed to be.
I know that
But it's too late now
For eyes to be lifted.
For a new sun to rise.
For black, white & grey to turn to colour.
The frightened child
Lives within the weakened man.
The heavy burden of being
Offering no sense of redemption.
If it all ends the same for all
And this is as good as it gets,
Don't delay me, I pray
Fast forward me to the end of the story.

Pandemic

The dark cloak of fear has wrapped itself
around,
Like nothing we have ever worn before.
The touch of hand in hand on which we
each depend
Is now that which threatens many most.
Locked alone inside our minds as well as
inside our homes.
Isolated. Remote.
Crippled by the uncertainty of what may
yet be to come.
But amid the grey we also have the black
and white
The clarity that health is all there is.
That we can fight the isolation, we can
open arms, we can face the fear.
Together.
We *can* reach out without having to touch.
If we all reach out together.
Who among us really needs to be alone?
If we all reach out together.
So think 'us' not 'you'
At least until the cloak is cast aside.
Whenever that may be.

The Promise I Made

Once upon a time, a whole life ago
I held you close and whispered
That I promised you the world.

And though my heart spoke truth to you
That pledge has not been honoured.
The promise undelivered.

Those words, I see now that they were hollow
Just like the man that I became.
An empty vessel, devoid of substance.

Because nothing that I have
Is anything you need.
For all I have is love.
And I'm not sure that's enough.

Life Is A Rollercoaster

Growing older and life speeds up
Like the downward slope of a rollercoaster
Without an upward curve to apply the brakes.
If he's truly honest
No joys completely compensate
For his life's inexorable journey home.
Inside the mind of the older man
The small child remains.
His childhood maybe past and yet
His need to feel protected
Has never gone away.
And then his evening starts to turn to night
And he prepares himself to be
Little more than someone else's memory;
A faded photograph on a mantelpiece
To be shown one day to a disinterested child.
That's when reality dawns
That there's no-one left to protect him anyway
And that the hand he really wants in his
Left some time ago itself.

Honesty

Do you hate me for who I am
Or who I failed to be?
The one who should have lifted you
Long after I'd bounced you on my knee.
Did I disappoint you
For not being all I should?
Semi-present on the sidelines
Rather than an ever-present force for good.
I may not have made your dreams come true
But believe, I've loved you nonetheless,
So, forgive me if you're able
For causing you distress.
I'm sensing my time may now be short
So, let's not leave anything unasked.
Please don't be sad or have regret
When you learn that I have passed.

Choose To Live

Supermarket flowers cling to a lamppost
As handwritten notes wilt in the falling rain.
What should be for lovers, for family and friends
Now the markers of a young life taken,
Another and then another.
Talking heads earnestly condemn
Until the circus moves on
Leaving hearts torn apart and hopes
forever unfulfilled.
How many more flowers
Against how many more walls?
How many more blood-stained broken dreams
On how many more tear-soaked notes?
Let the flowers be beautiful again.
Put the knives down and choose to live.

The Game of Life

Roll the dice
And play the game of Life,
Where risk and chance combine
To set our separate paths.
Take a card, make your move
Don't pass Go or you'll have to prove
That you have what it takes
To be true to yourself
To be an original
Not off the shelf.
Set your strategy, keep your eyes on the prize
Navigate the lows
So you can enjoy the highs.
But do it fast because time is short
And before you know it, you'll be caught.
That's when the game comes to an end
And away from the board, your soul will be sent.

Be More Kind

Empty places at dining tables
One-way chatter where there once was two.
Their presence sensed now, more than felt
But love unbroken between them and you.
Hear their laughter in the hollow
Smell their scent to bind you close.
A half-filled wine glass; a snatch of song
The thoughts that make you miss them most.
Grief cascades like crashing waves,
Sapped by sadness, too tired to sleep
The sheer enormity of what we've lost
We find ourselves too spent to weep.
Remember each that we are losing
Was a cherished soul, good and kind
All with family broken-hearted
Watch out for those they've left behind.
For each of us, our time will come
So, be someone who will be missed.
Spread love and hope and be more kind
So tears will flow when you're last kissed.

New Year's Resolution

For my New Year's Resolution
I plan to start a revolution,
For us to be more self-effacing
More humility to be embracing.
The world would be a better place
If fewer were so double-faced,
Accept your words can cause real pain
Rein it in and start again.
Not everything needs to earn acclaim
Get off your pedestal, help light the flame
Drop that attitude you show in spades
And instead, help man the barricades.

.

2020

One day you'll tell your kids of the year
When darkness shrouded the world
And chilled the stone-cold truth of fear.
When it cloaked us in our own confinement
Quarantined in a joyless existence,
Deprived of the human contact
That only a hug from a loved one brings.
When each warm home became its own bleak house,
Doors shut tight against those outside.
Who among us didn't battle demons
Just to reach our pillow every night?
And yet there came a flicker,
A tiny burst of light to illuminate the gloom.
And the fragile flame grew strong against the
blackness,
Bringing the hope, the promise
That smiles would finally
Cause our masks to fall.
It's still the early hours now
And it remains dark outside
But, as sure as night descends,
I now believe the sun will rise again.

Sundays

Sunday mornings
Should come with warnings
Not to sleep in for too long.

But Sunday evenings,
it has to be said,
As the new week approaches
tend to fill me with dread.

For if Sunday is Bond
Then Monday is Blofeld
I know he's been expecting me.

So, I try to stay calm
To offset the alarm
For what the week ahead may bring.

About Howard Robinson

In his writing, Howard Robinson enjoys taking ordinary people and placing them in extraordinary situations and playing around with the way they would respond. He says it brings out the megalomaniac in him.

He has four novels published – The Bitterest Pill; Micah Seven Five; The Sixth Republic and Know Your Own Darkness - and is currently working on his fifth.

He started writing almost as soon as he was able to. At first, they tended to be dodgy poems at primary school and then short stories that seemed to win the approval of teachers. His Modern History degree taught him the importance of structure in writing and of exploring language and his 35 plus year career in PR has given him the opportunity to write on the broadest possible range of subjects from car paintshops to nuts and bolts.

But essentially, Howard says he writes for himself. He tries to create stories he would enjoy reading, to explore situations and emotions safely within the confines of the page. He aims to create worlds and characters with whom readers can identify and sympathise.

He lives in London with his wife.

Printed in Great Britain
by Amazon

36188535R00024